HOCKEY CANADA

THE SENSATIONAL JAROME IGINLA

PETER BAILEY

D0557625

Fenn Publishing Company Ltd.
Bolton, Canada

Fenn Publishing Company Ltd.

THE SENSATIONAL JAROME IGINLA

A Fenn Publishing Book / First Published in 2006

We acknowledge the financial support of the Government of Canada through the Book Publishing Industry Development Program (BPIDP) for our publishing activities This book is licensed by Hockey Canada.

Designed by First Image
Fenn Publishing Company Ltd.
Bolton, Ontario, Canada
Printed in Canada

Library and Archives Canada Cataloguing in Publication

Bailey, Peter, 1962-

The sensational Jarome Iginla / Peter Bailey.

ISBN 1-55168-287-7

1. Iginla, Jarome, 1977-. 2. Hockey players--Canada--Biography. I. Title.

GV848.5.I35B34 2006   796.962'092   C2006-904754-5

Cover photos: Matthew Manor/Hockey Hall of Fame;
(*with trophy*) Dave Sandford/Hockey Hall of Fame

CONTENTS

PRELUDE

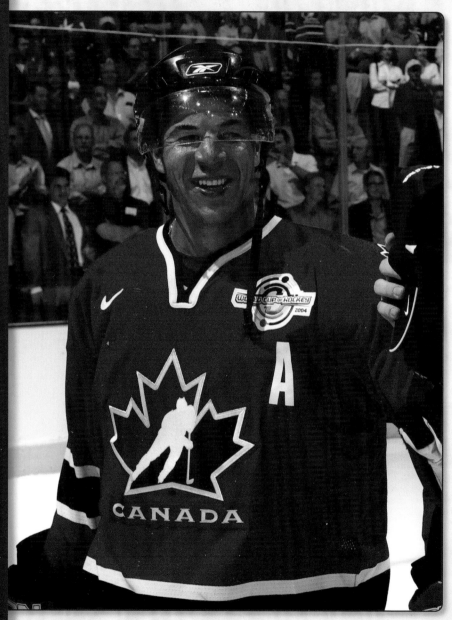

Always with a smile, Jarome is the perfect combination of competitor and sportsman.

In order to prepare as thoroughly as possible for the Olympic Winter Games in February 2002, Team Canada general manager Wayne Gretzky and his staff held a three-day summer orientation camp in August 2001 so that all the players who hoped to play for their country could meet each other and get to know the coaching staff. Jarome Iginla was not part of that group of players to be invited. No. He just wasn't that big a superstar in a country that produced more great players than any other in the world.

That didn't upset Jarome. It didn't even make him mad, or discouraged. It motivated him. It inspired him to work even harder for the upcoming season because Wayne had also said that anyone who had a great start to the new year would be considered for the team when the final names were announced just before Christmas 2001.

But then Jarome got lucky. Just before the mini-camp opened, one of the players scheduled to go, Simon Gagne, suffered an injury and couldn't attend. Jarome was called in as a last-minute replacement. Those three quick days playing with Mario Lemieux and the other greats of the game made a huge difference to Jarome. Still, he was not guaranteed a place on the final roster.

To make clear his desires to represent Canada at the Olympics, Jarome began the NHL's regular season incredibly well. By the time Wayne named Canada's 2002 Olympic team in December, Jarome was leading the league in scoring and was "one of the best players in the league," according to the Great One. Jarome was named to Team Canada for the Olympics.

CHAPTER ONE

ONE GOAL IN MIND

Jarome flies down the wing with only one thing in mind—go to the net.

> "When he was nine, he told me he was going to be a professional hockey player."
>
> *Jarome's mom, Susan*

The full name of the great player we all know as Jarome Iginla is—get ready for this!—Arthur-Leigh Elvis Adekunle Jarome Jij Junior Iginla. This is a name that represents everything great about Canada. Jarome's father came from Nigeria. The name Iginla in Yoruba (a language in that country) means "big tree," which is certainly what Jarome became—on ice and off.

When Jarome's father arrived in Canada, he decided to change his name from Adekunle to something traditionally North American. He saw Elvis Presley singing and thought it was a common name! "He thought it was like Mike or Mark. He didn't realize who Elvis was," Jarome admitted.

Well, Elvis came to Canada at age 18 and hoped to become a doctor. He met a woman named Susan Schuchard who was born in Oregon and was hoping to become a jazz singer. Susan was one of eight children. Her parents, Rick and Frances, were schoolteachers. They came up to Edmonton in 1968 for a two-year assignment to help St. Albert overcome a teacher shortage. St. Albert was a small town just outside Edmonton. The Schuchard family loved the city so much that they never went back to Oregon.

"My mom had to work a lot to support me for sports and different activities"

Elvis and Susan fell in love, got married, and settled in Edmonton where Jarome was born on Canada Day 1977 (July 1). The parents stopped living together when Jarome was just a year old. Susan moved back close to her parents in St. Albert, and Jarome was raised by the three adults who took special care of him.

As a boy, young Jarome was very active. In the winter he enjoyed playing hockey, but in the summer it was baseball and later golf. "My mom had to work a lot to support me for sports and different activities," Jarome explained. "My grandparents helped out where they could and took me to a lot of practices, and I always had somebody in the stands. I always had somebody there," he repeated, stressing the importance for a child to have a relative watching him play a game and supporting him.

"Bless his heart," his grandfather, Rick said. "All I did was tie his skates. Oh, and teach him the wraparound," he said with a smile, referring to the move where a player swings out from behind the goal to slide the puck into the net past the surprised goalie.

"As a little guy," Rick, told, "Jarome would come with me to baseball games and shag balls. He loved to be active. He loved baseball and he could make up to $20 a day, fifty cents a ball." Jarome made this money by collecting the foul balls and long home run balls hit by the players.

Jarome was surrounded by love and support during his childhood. His mother worked as a massage therapist and his father decided to go to the University of Alberta to study law (instead of medicine). So, it was his grandparents who did much of taking care of the young boy. Also, because Jarome had plenty of energy, his mom got him involved in everything. He played tennis and baseball, went bowling, and even studied music. "My family's very musical," Jarome revealed. "On my mom's side, my grandma runs a music school in St. Albert and my mother's going to school studying to be a drama teacher."

Jarome grew up admiring Wayne Gretzky, Mark Messier, and the Edmonton Oilers, and why wouldn't he? The years he was a kid—the 1980s—were the years the Oilers were winning all their Stanley Cups. "I think he chose hockey," his granddad went on, "because he was able to play it year 'round. He was good at it."

But Jarome also admired the game because of players such as Tony McKegney and Claude Vilgrain, and he was especially proud of Grant Fuhr. All of those players were black, playing

*As a kid, Jarome admired these Stanley Cup-winning
Edmonton Oilers teams of the mid-1980s.*

The great Grant Fuhr makes a patented glove save.

in the NHL at a time when only a few non-white players were in the league. That has changed now. "When I was younger, I was aware there weren't many black players in the NHL, and it meant a lot to me to see Grant Fuhr starring in the NHL and knowing it was possible to reach my dream," Jarome said.

That dream started when he was just six years old. "I started in Grade 2," Jarome told of his humble hockey beginnings. "I went with my aunt and her boyfriend to an arena, an outdoor rink which was a block away from my grandparents. My grandpa... was happy to get me involved in it. My dad didn't know too much about hockey, and my mom didn't really know much about it, either."

Ah, yes, The Dream. Ever since Jarome started skating and playing in a league he wanted to become an NHL player. When he was just ten years old, he was invited to participate in a summer all-star program run by Bill Comrie. Bill owned The Brick furniture stores and he had a son about Jarome's age. Mike Comrie also went on to play in the NHL. "From my first day of going to junior school, I knew I would make it," Jarome said proudly of his NHL dream.

"When he was nine, he told me he was going to be a professional hockey player," his mom revealed. Said granddad: "He had a dream, and with hard work he made that dream come true."

Jarome took the game very seriously, and when he was 14 he started to lift weights to add muscle and strength to his body. That year, he played provincial junior hockey with the St. Albert Blazers, and even though he was only 14, he was a star player right away. What made it even more special to play at St. Alberts was that his mother was the team's anthem singer! It was her lovely voice that sang O Canada prior to each Blazers game. If that couldn't make Jarome play well, nothing could.

Hockey was Jarome's true love, and he was too good a player not to be noticed by other teams and coaches. In his first year with the team, he averaged more than a point a game, and after his second year he averaged one goal and two points per game. As a result, teams in major junior hockey were starting to take notice of a rising star. In the summer of 1993, Jarome was drafted by the Kamloops Blazers into the Western Hockey League (WHL). As soon as he agreed to play in this league, a league intended to train players for the NHL, Jarome never gave a thought to anything but becoming a star player in his dream league.

CHAPTER TWO

MAKING THE NHL GRADE

A teenage Jarome started playing serious hockey with Kamloops in the WHL.

"I came off the plane and they told me I would be playing."

Jarome recalling how he got into his first NHL game.

The next three years were vital to the way Jarome learned to play the game. As he had done all his life, he learned from every game he played and he got better and better. The adjustment from St. Alberts to Kamloops was enormous for him, though. First, the players were all older, stronger, faster and possessed greater skills. Second, he was now living in British Columbia, far from his mother and grandparents. Third, he didn't play well or very often when he first joined Kamloops. And, fourth, he was playing on one of the best teams in the league, which was both good and bad. Good because he got to learn from and play with the best players in the WHL; bad because he still had a long way to go before he could consider himself as good as most of his teammates.

"It was tough leaving home at 16 years old and not playing a lot," he admitted. "I was sitting on the bench, getting two shifts a period." Despite his early lack of success, Jarome tried hard every chance he got. No matter how sad he became because of a lack of ice time, his mother and grandparents supported him from a distance. "They were always so positive," he said. "I never heard once that I had a bad game from them."

> *No matter how sad he became because of a lack of ice time, his mother and grandparents supported him from a distance.*

Jarome improved a great deal as that first year went on. By the playoffs, he was in the lineup every night, playing hard and contributing. The Blazers went on to win the Memorial Cup, the highest junior honour in Canada, after a tough series against Chicoutimi, Laval, and North Bay. They won all four playoff games they played. When Jarome came to training camp to start the 1994-95 season, he was himself bigger, stronger, more mature, and better prepared to handle the challenges of junior hockey.

Jarome scored just six goals in his first year but in his second season he scored an incredible 33 goals. As well, he went from

33 penalty minutes to 111, an indication that he was starting to play like a power forward—a more physical game. When he was 16, he wasn't able to do this. Now, older and stronger, he could use his size and strength to play better.

In the 1995 WHL playoffs, Jarome was an even greater force and had a more important role in the team's second straight Memorial Cup championship. Winning this championship twice in a row is rare, indeed. Jarome had developed into such a good player so quickly that in the summer of 1995 he was selected by the Dallas Stars 11th overall at the NHL Entry Draft, an incredibly high choice. When he attended the draft in his hometown of Edmonton and heard his name called out, his dream had come true. He was on his way to the NHL!

Jarome attended training camp with the Stars that September, but the trip was supposed to be a learning experience and not his next career move. All that the team wanted now was for him to experience an NHL camp, play for a while with the best players, and then go back to Kamloops to learn more about how to play the game. So, after playing with Dallas players for a month, Jarome returned to the Blazers and focused on improving every aspect of his game. The Stars felt he needed to become a better skater, so he worked on that. He wanted to improve his diet and conditioning, so he focused on what he ate and how he trained. The talented boy was becoming a disciplined, intelligent young man.

When he arrived to begin his third year in Kamloops, Jarome was now a leader. He was 18 years old and an experienced WHL player, and he led by example. Over the course of this '95-'96 season, several important events turned him into a man. First, through no fault of his own, his NHL rights were traded. The Calgary Flames had Joe Nieuwendyk

As a member of the Blazers, Jarome developed into one of the best junior-aged players in all of Canada.

A determined Jarome gets knocked over in the slot,
but he still keeps his eye on the puck.

on the team, but he and the general manager could not agree on a new contract. The Flames traded the unhappy player to Dallas, and in return Dallas gave up Jarome and Corey Millen. The Stars were happy because they acquired a star scorer, and the Flames were happy because they got one of the top prospects in all of hockey—Jarome.

Calgary general manager Al Coates made the trade because, "His [Joe's] relationship with the organization had broken down. He wasn't going to play for us anymore...We knew [Jarome] would play in the league, and we knew he would be a good player."

What was funny about the deal was that when he was a kid, Jarome cheered for Edmonton, the team everyone in

Jarome was drafted by Dallas in 1995, one of the most exciting days of his life.

Calgary hated the most. Back then, he loved it when his Oilers beat the Flames. Now, he was going to do everything he could to help the Flames beat the Oilers!

At the time of this trade, December 19, 1995, Jarome was at the training camp for Team Canada's national junior team that was preparing to play in the World Junior Championship. That tournament was going to be played in Boston, Massachusetts, starting the day after Christmas. Only the best of the best juniors in the whole country were invited, and by this time it was clear Jarome was in this category of player.

> "We knew [Jarome] would play in the league, and we knew he would be a good player."

Canada had won gold at the World Junior Championships in 1993, 1994, and 1995, so there was plenty of pressure for the team to win again in 1996. The Canadians started out on the right foot by beating USA 6-1 in the first game of the tournament. Jarome set up two of the goals in the third period. Three days later, against Finland, he scored a goal and assist in a narrow 3-1 win. Later in the tournament he recorded a hat trick against the Ukraine.

Jarome saved his biggest moment for the biggest game, however. On January 3, 1996, he scored the winning goal in a 4-3 win over arch-rivals Russia in the semi-finals. This meant the team advanced to play for the championship again. In the gold-medal game, he again was the star, assisting on three of Canada's four goals in a 4-1 win over Sweden. Canada won its fourth straight gold at the World Juniors. Jarome was named the Best Forward in the tournament, leading all players with 12 points in six games.

> *He signed his first NHL contract just hours before stepping onto the ice for his first game.*

After the celebrations, Jarome returned to Kamloops to help his team the rest of the year. He ended the season scoring 63 goals in as many games, and he finished fourth in the WHL with 136 total points. Although Kamloops was eliminated from the Memorial Cup playoffs, the Calgary Flames were in the middle of the Stanley Cup playoffs and called him up to play! He signed his first NHL contract just hours before stepping onto the ice for his first game. "I came off the plane and they told me I would be playing," he related about how he found out about his initial NHL appearance.

Jarome played the night of April 21, 1996, at home to Chicago. The Blackhawks were leading the best-of-seven series 2-0, and in this third game they won 7-5. Jarome recorded a third-period assist while playing on the team's number-one

Starting out in the NHL, Jarome was no different, trying to position himself in front of the enemy goalie to screen him or deflect a shot.

line with Theo Fleury and German Titov. Two nights later, Chicago won again, this time 2-1 in triple overtime. Although that last loss eliminated the Flames, Jarome scored the only Calgary goal!

He played well enough and looked so mature and calm during the tense playoffs that the team made sure he had played his last game of junior hockey. Jarome Iginla was now an NHL player.

BREAKOUT SEASON

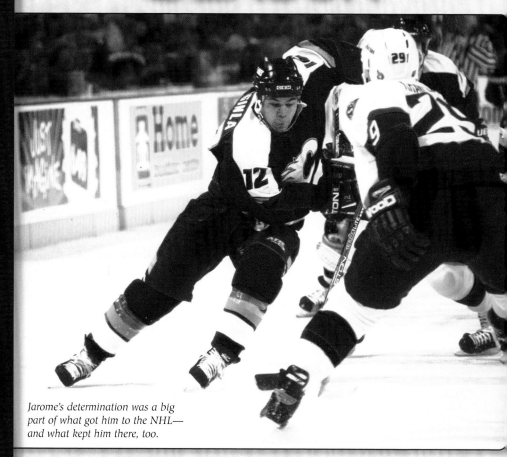

Jarome's determination was a big part of what got him to the NHL—and what kept him there, too.

CHAPTER THREE

"He really understands all the facets of the game."

Jarome's linemate, Dave Gagner

Most players who go from junior to the NHL have a difficult time adjusting at first. The majority of NHLers are mature men, bigger, faster, stronger, and smarter. As Jarome noticed, "In junior, you get that extra split second, and sometimes that can make a big difference."

Jarome's challenge was even greater because he was now with Calgary and expected to replace Joe Nieuwendyk. Joe had helped Calgary win the Stanley Cup in 1989, so he was an important player on the team and to the fans of the Flames.

As well, Jarome was such a star at the World Junior Championship and had such a great finish to the season with Kamloops. Everyone now expected him to not just to make the team but to be one of the stars. If Jarome had any difficulty adapting to the NHL in his first full season, however, he sure didn't show it. For starters, he played every one of the team's 82 games in the 1996-97 season. This proved that he was emotionally and physically ready to play in the NHL. Jarome also led all NHL rookies with 50 points and was third in goals with 21.

> *"He really understands all the facets of the game—going into the corners, playing the power play, everything,"*

"He really understands all the facets of the game—going into the corners, playing the power play, everything," his linemate Dave Gagner said.

Jarome used his experiences in Kamloops to adjust in Calgary. "My first Memorial Cup, I was very nervous," he explained. "My second one, I wasn't nearly as nervous. This is the same thing...I think at first I was a bit too cautious. I just gave guys too much respect." Then, once he realized his mistake, Jarome played in the NHL as though he belonged in the league, not like he was just lucky to be there.

Jarome played most of the year on a line with Dave Gagner, a veteran player, and a rookie, Jonas Hoglund. This was a careful plan by coach Pierre Page. He wanted the energy and skill of the two rookies to go with the experience of the older player to create a threesome that was skilled and smart at the same time. "He really pushes us and makes us ready to play," Jarome said of Dave. "If we start to slack off for a shift, he's there to remind us to get it in gear."

Jarome's great play as a rookie saw him finish second in voting for the Calder Trophy. Still, despite his contributions, the team didn't make the playoffs. As he always did during his life, Jarome turned a negative into a positive when he accepted an invitation to play for Team Canada at the senior World Championship in Finland. This is a tournament that is always scheduled during the NHL playoffs, so only NHL players who miss the playoffs are able to participate.

Nonetheless, Jarome's teammates at this tournament included Chris Pronger, Owen Nolan, and Mark Recchi. Jarome started the series off on the right foot, assisting on Canada's first goal of the championship. In his next game, he scored a goal against Tommy Salo of Sweden, and right after that he counted another against Latvia. In the team's fourth game, against USA, Jarome kept his point streak alive with another assist, this time on a goal by Rob Zamuner. In a 6-0 win over Italy, he had his third assist of the tournament.

In all, he had five points and was a +6, second best on the team. Canada won the gold medal in the best-of-three finals against Sweden, and Jarome had another top medal from international hockey to go with his World Junior Championship gold from the previous year. This was a huge accomplishment.

Jarome's first years were a time of adjustment to a bigger and faster game.

Jarome knew how important it was to follow the play and keep his eye on the puck.

Jarome lets go a mighty slapshot.

Jarome wore number 12 the first chance he got, the same number he liked in junior.

Many great players over the years have suffered something called the Sophomore Jinx. It's not a disease or sickness. It's an expression that refers to a player's second year in the NHL when things don't go as well as the first year. The player arrives to training camp and figures that after his initial jump to the big time he'll have no trouble continuing to improve. Wrong. Jarome found out the hard way that the only way to improve is to work harder and harder and never think that success in the past will guarantee success in the future. He didn't play as well as he could have in his second year, but it also didn't help that the team was going through a bad time as a whole. In fact, for all of '97-'98, the Flames had a weak record of 26-41-15 and missed the playoffs.

As a result, when Jarome showed up to training camp for his third season, his coach, Brian Sutter, was hard on him from the very first day. He wanted to motivate the young star to perform the way he knew Jarome could. "He talked to me last season and in the off-season," Jarome said of his preparation with coach Sutter. "He wants me to come play every night, and he wants me to be more aggressive. That's fair. I didn't have that enough last year. Offensively, he told me, he wants me to produce. The biggest thing he wants is for me to compete with more of an edge."

What this meant was that the coach wanted Jarome to play a more physical and confident game. The previous year, he scored just 13 goals. Coach Sutter knew that Jarome was capable of so much more. He was going to give Jarome the chance to score more, but in return he expected Jarome to play with more energy.

Jarome screens Toronto goalie Curtis Joseph.

*Jarome skates by the much larger
Boston defenceman Hal Gill.*

Like Mark Messier, Jarome lets go a snap shot on his off wing, his back foot off the ice for better balance and strength.

Jarome skates through the middle of the ice looking for a pass.

This combination of pressure and support was exactly what Jarome needed. He more than doubled his goals to 28. This was the best on the team. Still, though, Jarome had few players around him to contribute, and the Flames again missed the playoffs. The next year, Jarome increased his point total to 63, another indication that he was improving all the time. He even had a 16-game point streak at one time, which was best in the entire NHL that season.

It was in 2000-01 that the world really started to see what Jarome could do. He scored 31 goals, another career best, and his 71 points was also tops on the team. Jarome had now played five years in the NHL and had improved steadily. He knew what it took to win and play hard. He knew he had the talent to be not just a regular player but a real superstar. And now, at age 24, he was ready to take his position as one of the best players in the world.

During the year he was made assistant captain, which was a sign that the team wanted him to be a leader both in the dressing room and on the ice. He also made an important decision off ice as well. He announced that for every goal he scored he would donate $1,000 to KidSport Calgary, a charity in his adopted home. Jarome was starting to be a player the team needed, not the other way around.

And now, at age 24, he was ready to take his position as one of the best players in the world.

CANADIAN GOLD

Jarome celebrates his Olympic gold medal with Simon Gagne (left) and Joe Sakic (middle).

"Jarome Iginla right now
may be the best forward
in the NHL."

Wayne Gretzky

Jarome's life and career changed forever one September night in 2001. He was out at a restaurant having dinner with friends in Edmonton when his girlfriend called him on his cell phone. Wayne Gretzky called, she said. Are you joking? He asked. No, she said. You'd better call him.

Jarome called Wayne, and the Great One said that Simon Gagne had hurt his shoulder and couldn't go to Calgary for Team Canada's mini-training camp in preparation for the Olympics. Could Jarome fill in? Uh, yes! He was on his way to Calgary by the end of the night. The next morning he was at the team's orientation camp. The surprise call was maybe the best way for him to have gotten the invitation. "In some ways," Jarome explained, "the last-minute call was good because I didn't get too much time to get too nervous about it—and I would have been nervous for sure."

For the next four days, he played with the best skaters in all of Canada, the ones who hoped to represent their country at the 2002 Olympics in February, just five months from then. He played with Mario Lemieux, said hello to Joe Sakic, goofed around with the puck with Steve Yzerman, took shots on Martin Brodeur. It was unbelievable.

> *It was more mental, being out there with the best players in the game, competing alongside them.*

"It definitely helped me," Jarome said of that amazing experience. "It wasn't as much getting my legs going and skating at that speed. It was more mental, being out there with the best players in the game, competing alongside them. It helped my confidence, helped me see what the next level is at and motivated me to try and get there."

The Calgary Flames noticed a difference right away when he re-joined the team at its NHL training camp. Jarome played more aggressively and drove hard to the net every shift. By the time the 2001-02 season was 12 games old, the Calgary

Jarome sporting Calgary's third sweater, much different from the traditional logo.

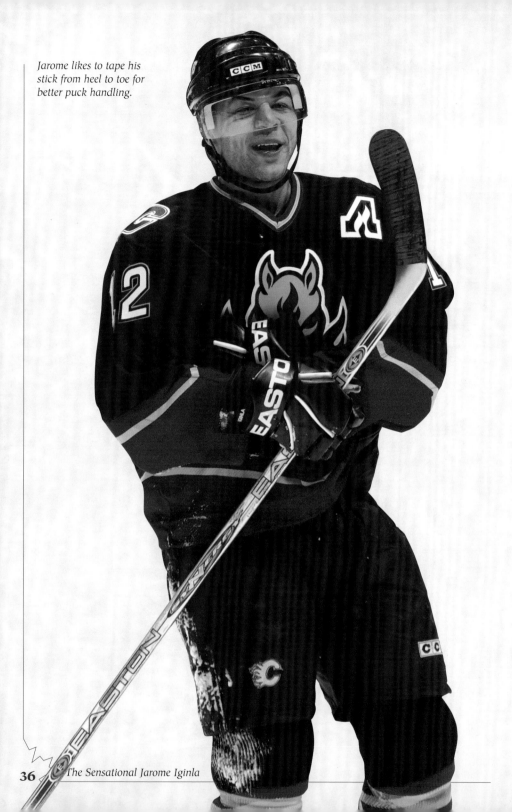

Jarome likes to tape his stick from heel to toe for better puck handling.

Flames were on a roll. They lost only two of those games, and Jarome had 19 points, tops in the entire league. The team's goalie, Miikka Kiprusoff, was also playing really well, but it was Jarome who was the star. Wayne Gretzky said it simplest when he publicly declared that, "Jarome Iginla right now may be the best forward in the NHL."

Wow. Jarome was amazed. "I couldn't believe it," he said when he heard of the complimentary words from Wayne. "That was very kind of him to say that. I looked up to him as a kid. He was the best player ever and that was a huge compliment and a huge thrill."

Not only that, but it was clear that when Wayne made this comment he was also saying that Jarome was going to be named to Team Canada's Olympic roster. Sure enough, in December 2001, Jarome's name was on the final list. The little kid from St. Albert, Alberta, was on his way to represent Canada at the Olympics in hockey! Jarome continued to lead the entire NHL in scoring right up to the time that the league shut down so the players could go to Salt Lake and participate in the Olympics.

Jarome and the team arrived in Salt Lake just a couple of days before their first game. They practiced a few times and talked a lot about how they wanted to play. They planned on winning gold for Canada, and they wanted to make sure their preparation was excellent.

In Canada's first game, against Sweden, Jarome played on a line with two great members of the Detroit Red Wings, Steve Yzerman and Brendan Shanahan. The threesome didn't have much success, though, and the team lost 5-2, not a good way to start. Nonetheless, with players such as Mario Lemieux in the dressing room, no one worried about that score once the game was over. That game was over and there was another one to prepare for.

The second game, against Germany, saw Jarome play with Steve Yzerman and Simon Gagne, and this line was more effective. The team won 3-2 to give the players some confidence. The next game was a very impressive 3-3 tie with the Czech Republic, one of the top teams in the Olympics. The tie set up a quarter-finals elimination game against Finland.

In that game, Jarome played on another line, this time with Simon Gagne and Joe Sakic. Coach Pat Quinn was moving Jarome around trying to find that perfect combination. Although Jarome's line didn't contribute a goal in this big game, Canada won 2-1 to advance to the semi-finals. One more game to a gold-medal showdown!

The score in the semi-finals wasn't close. Canada clobbered Belarus 7-1, and the last goal for Canada was scored by Jarome. He shot right away after taking a nice pass from Brendan Shanahan to record his first goal and point of the tournament, and he headed to the gold-medal game against USA full of confidence.

Jarome wasn't just a small part of the team that beat USA 5-2 to win an Olympic gold medal—he was an essential part of the victory. The first period of that game was played at lightning speed by both teams. As the first 20 minutes drew to a close, the score was tied 1-1. But, with less than two minutes to go, Joe Sakic tore down the right wing and held on to the puck while his centreman, number 12 Jarome Iginla, raced to the net at full speed. Jarome was being checked by an American defenceman, but he kept on going hard to the net. Just as Jarome reached the crease, Joe drilled a hard pass to his stick and Jarome tipped the puck past goalie Mike Richter to give Canada a 2-1 lead after one period. It was a huge goal.

The Sensational Jarome Iginla

Jarome beats USA goalie Mike Richter in the gold-medal game of the 2002 Olympics.

Jarome is mobbed by Steve Yzerman after the goal.

Jarome poses with Simon Gagne and their 2002 Olympic gold medals from Salt Lake City, Utah.

Back with the Flames, Jarome continued his great play for the rest of the 2001-02 season.

In the second period, the Americans tied the score, but later in the period Joe Sakic put Canada ahead 3-2. As the teams skated out to start the third period, Canada knew it was just 20 minutes away from an historic gold medal. The players also knew that the USA team wasn't going to give up.

The most incredible goal of the game, maybe of the entire Olympics, occurred late in the third. For 16 minutes Canada held the Americans at bay and continued to lead 3-2. And for 16 minutes the Americans tried everything to tie the score. Then, Jarome got the puck down the right wing and tore in over the American blueline. Like a bull, he skated straight for the goal. You could see by his eyes that no one was going to stop him. He looked straight at goalie Mike Richter as he skated in. As he reached the crease, Jarome drilled a shot to the far side of the net that beat the goalie cleanly. Every player on the Canadian bench jumped for joy! With a 4-2 lead and less than four minutes to go, gold was now assured for Canada.

Like a bull, he skated straight for the goal. You could see by his eyes that no one was going to stop him.

Joe Sakic scored once more three minutes later, and Canada went on to win the gold medal with a 5-2 win. Jarome scored two goals and was one of the best players on the ice. As he accepted his gold medal and sang O Canada with his teammates, he was practically crying with joy and delight. The little kid who always dreamed of playing in the NHL was now standing arm-in-arm with the 23 best hockey players in the world.

One little-known story from the Olympics, far from the ice and the gold medal, occurred at a little restaurant downtown Salt Lake City. Jarome went out for dinner with a small group of Team Canada teammates. He met some students from Calgary who travelled to Salt Lake to watch the hockey games even though they had nowhere to stay. Jarome left the table for a few minutes and came back with a hotel reservation, fully paid, for the students. That move was as classy as any breakaway pass or overtime goal any player could ever score.

Jarome returned to Calgary and was given a hero's welcome. He also continued his excellent play with the Flames for the rest of the season. It was a frustrating time for him, though, because although he kept scoring and scoring, the team couldn't put together a big winning streak to get into the playoffs.

Another big personal moment for Jarome came on April 7, 2002, near the end of the regular season. That night he scored his 50th goal of the season, the only NHL player to reach this milestone this year. He became the first Calgary player to reach 50 since Gary Roberts in 1991-92. It was a typical Jarome goal. "[Craig Conroy] sent me in on the wing," Jarome described, "and going in I thought this might be the one. I was putting my head down just trying to shoot it as hard as I could. I tried to go high glove, and fortunately it found the net."

Later in the same game, Jarome scored again, but this is how the season went. Even though he scored two goals in the game, the Flames lost 3-2 to Chicago. Jarome scored one more goal before the season ended. He finished with the best points totals in the league. His 52 goals was tops, earning him the Rocket Richard Trophy. His 96 points was also number one, meaning he had won the Art Ross Trophy. And, after the season, the players from around the league voted Jarome the best player in the NHL by awarding him the Lester B. Pearson Award.

"When he came back from the Olympics," linemate Craig Conroy explained, "he'd been on centre stage with all those great players and he was able to contribute and be a factor. Ever since then, he's kind of taken it to a new level."

Jarome fights off a check from future Hall of Fame defenceman Al MacInnis and makes a nice pass.

An Established Superstar

CHAPTER FIVE

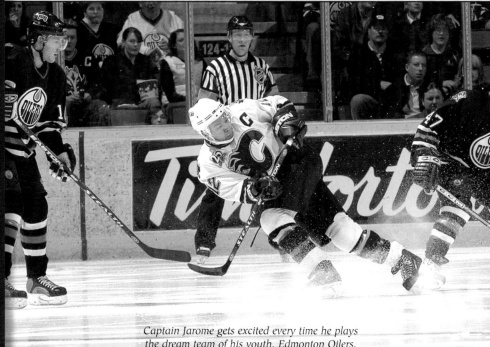

*Captain Jarome gets excited every time he plays
the dream team of his youth, Edmonton Oilers.*

*"I've decided to let Jarome
be the captain this year."*

Teammate Craig Conroy

Jarome entered the 2002-03 season with a more confident attitude than ever before. He was now entering his seventh NHL season. He had won a gold medal at the Olympics with Canada. He was a 50-goal scorer and the top point getter in the entire league. At 25 years of age, he was at the peak of his playing abilities. Over the summer, he ran his first ever hockey school in Calgary, which was, of course, a huge success. He got engaged to girlfriend Kara Kirkland, a physiotherapist whom he had known since he was 13. He also signed a new contract with the Flames which ensured he would play in Calgary for at least two more years.

"Last year was a good year," he said, assessing his career moving forward, "but I think I can be a better player. I'm going to push myself to do that and have a better year."

Everything was in place for Jarome to go to even greater heights, but the one thing you can never gauge in the development of a player or the way plans unfold is the burden of expectation. The truth is, the previous year no one expected Jarome to do what he did, so it was a pleasant surprise when he accomplished so much. This season, he was supposed to score 50 goals, win the scoring championship, and lead his team to the playoffs. That was a far more difficult task.

> *For no apparent reason, Jarome started the year off slowly. Then he ran into injury troubles.*

For no apparent reason, Jarome started the year off slowly. Then he ran into injury troubles. He scored just four times in his first 21 games. A year earlier he had 19 goals in the same period. Shots that went in last year were hitting the post this year. Breakaways last year that were beautiful goals turned into highlight-reel saves by the goalies this year.

"I've hit a lot of posts and I've missed a lot of breakaways," he admitted. "But, you know, you can only hit so many goal posts.

Jarome brought both calm and energy to his role as Calgary's captain.

You're just an inch off. At some point they'll start going in. I've also had more breakaways than I've ever had in my life. Hopefully, some of those will start going in, too."

To make matters worse, he suffered a hip injury, and a groin injury, and his hand was so swollen at one point that he couldn't even put his Team Canada gold medal ring on his finger. He saw the trainer's room as much as the dressing room and it seemed as if he were playing hurt all the time. "It hasn't gone the way anyone would have liked," he agreed just before Christmas of the way the new year had started. "There's still two-thirds of the season left. I'm optimistic things will turn around for the team and myself."

"This team needs Jarome," he added. "He's the franchise and we're behind him 110%."

As it turned out, Jarome did have a better second half than first. He played in his second straight All-Star Game, this time for the West, and he even earned an assist in the game. Still, his performance in Calgary wasn't enough to get the team into the playoffs, and that was what was most important of all. He finished with 35 goals and 67 points. These were decent personal numbers, but the Flames missed the chase for the Stanley Cup for the sixth straight season.

Teammate and captain Craig Conroy understood Jarome's position. "He hasn't been 100 per cent all year," Craig said. "There's a lot of pressure on him. There have been so many situations that aren't his fault. He's had opportunities and goalies have played well against him. This team needs Jarome," he added. "He's the franchise and we're behind him 110 per cent."

To back up his words, Craig made an amazing gesture prior to the start of the 2003-04 season. It was a change that had a significant impact on the course of the team. On October 8, 2003, just before the start of the new season, Craig took the "C" off his sweater and gave it to Jarome. "I've been talking to Jarome

"He's such a great player, a leader, everything. It's time for him to take over this team..."

for a month or so about the captaincy," Craig revealed. "We've been discussing everything. I talked to [coach] Darryl Sutter and I talked to Jarome. I've decided to let Jarome be the captain this year. Jarome has matured. He's such a great player, a leader, everything. It's time for him to take over this team...This decision is the best one for the team."

Jarome was happy but humbled by the gesture. "It's a huge honour and thrill," he said with his trademark smile. "It means a lot to me that he [Craig] wants me to wear it. I've been given a little more leadership this year, and I've taken a little more leadership. I've been here for a while. I've been through some of the downs. We're ready for ups."

Jarome's coach Darryl Sutter was very supportive of the change. "Jarome is a quality young man and a terrific hockey player whom people look up to," he agreed. "His work ethic and commitment to being the best are examples of how all players should prepare and compete."

Jarome responded in kind to the compliments. "I have been very lucky to have played with many great captains that I have learned from over the course of my career...I'm ready for the next challenge and the responsibilities that go with it."

Jarome had played well in training camp with linemates Craig Conroy and Dean McAmmond, but now as the captain he knew his and the team's attitude had to change as well. Second best was no longer acceptable. "We've been in a rebuilding cycle and cycles take time," he suggested, "but this year, absolutely anything less than making the playoffs would be a huge disappointment...I think we're more stable and can play more confidently and can win more games than we have in the past."

Jarome backed up his words, played like the captain, and got his team off to a great start to the '03-'04 season. At

Jarome makes a move and maintains control of the puck.

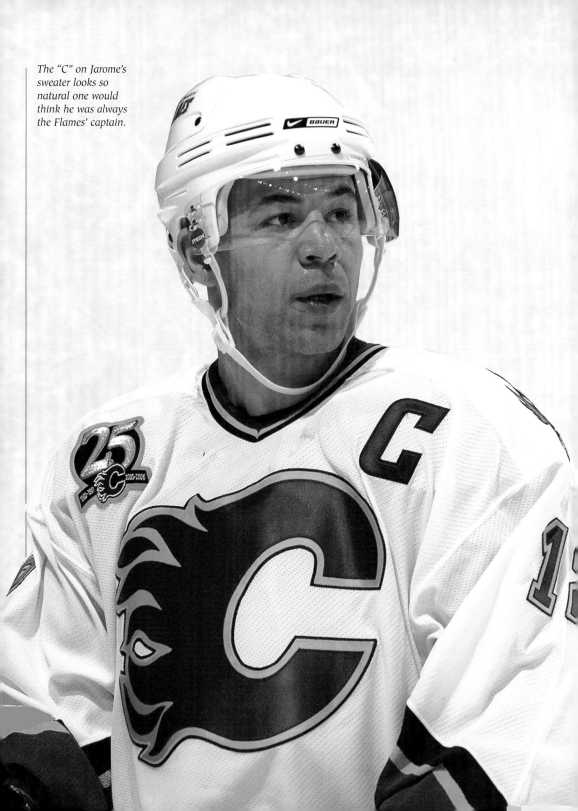

The "C" on Jarome's sweater looks so natural one would think he was always the Flames' captain.

the back end, goalie Miikka Kiprusoff, whom everyone called "Kipper," was providing the team with amazing goaltending as well. The Flames were playing only .500 hockey through the first two months, but Jarome was scoring and none of the team's losses were lop-sided. So long as they were competitive every night, they knew their chances of making the playoffs were excellent.

As well, they beat Toronto and Montreal in consecutive games in mid-December to give them a bit of confidence. This was a time they usually played so poorly they took themselves out of playoff contention. Instead, the Flames used these wins to go on a long streak of good fortune. They posted a record of 13-3-3 from the time of the wins over the Habs and Leafs through to the end of the year. As Calgary started 2004, it was a team on the rise, playing with confidence, and getting great goaltending.

"If he's not there, we don't win," Jarome said of Miikka during their great run in December. "I think my season has been good, but Kipper has allowed only two goals a night. He's been there for us."

Jarome played in his third straight All-Star Game in February 2004 in Minnesota, an honour that recognized his value to the Flames and the league. By the end of the regular season, Calgary had a record of 42-30-7-3 for 94 points, its best season in a decade. The Flames had made the playoffs, and Jarome's total of 41 goals was tied for the best in the league with Ilya Kovalchuk of Atlanta and Rick Nash of Columbus. Not only was Jarome back in top form, the Flames were in the playoffs for the first time since his first NHL games some eight years ago.

Now that the team was in the chase for Lord Stanley's Cup, however, the stakes were much higher and the task more difficult. The Flames had a first-round date with the Vancouver

> *The Flames had made the playoffs, and Jarome's total of 41 goals was tied for the best in the league ...*

Canucks, the team that had finished first in the Northwest Division. This was a test to see how far Jarome had come and whether the "C" really meant something to him and the team.

"It's been a long time for them," Jarome said of the team's fans who had waited so long to see playoff hockey again. "A lot of tough years, lean years, where it's been hard cheering for a non-playoff team." He promised to do more in the playoffs, and, boy, was he about to deliver.

The superior regular season by Vancouver meant that the Canucks had home ice advantage in the series. In Game 1, they used this advantage to the fullest, skating away with an impressive 5-3 win. After the loss, coach Sutter demanded that his captain step up, and in Game 2 that's exactly what Jarome did. He scored the first goal of the game when he took the puck from behind the Vancouver goal and wristed a high shot over the shoulder of goalie Dan Cloutier who was screened on the play. "I just waited a bit and had a lot of net to shoot at," Jarome said after the game. He was the dominant player all night, setting up several other scoring chances and playing a physical game as well. "I thought he played with some emotion," the coach agreed. "That's important. You have to have emotional leaders."

The victory gave the Flames reason to believe that they could win this series. The teams exchanged wins in Calgary to set up a crucial Game 5 in Vancouver. The winner of that game would take a huge 3-2 lead in the best-of-seven series. Jarome led the way in that game, assisting on the team's first goal by Craig Conroy and then scoring the winning goal early in the third period of a 2-1 win. He was leading not only with his words in the dressing room but with his actions on ice as well. "It was a tough game and to be on the verge of winning this series is a great feeling," he said after the game.

However, nothing worth doing is ever easy. In Game 6, the Canucks stormed the Calgary end and jumped into a big

Jarome keeps control of the puck behind the net, waiting
for a man to go to the slot for a quick pass.

4-0 lead. The Flames, however, refused to give up and they scored four goals to send the game into overtime. Brendan Morrison scored the winner for Vancouver to force Game 7, a heartbreaking loss after that great comeback. But the Flames were sure they could still win the last game, even if it were to be played in British Columbia and not Alberta.

Here's what defines Jarome Iginla. The scene is a restaurant in Vancouver the night after Game 6 and the night before Game 7. He and several players went to a nice eatery for dinner. Also in the restaurant was a family celebrating a wedding. One small boy in that party noticed Jarome but was too shy to say anything until the players had finished eating and were getting ready to go. Then the small boy called out, "Gook luck, Iggy."

> *"Gook luck, Iggy."*

Jarome turned and saw the young fan at a table. He left his teammates and went over to say hello. He signed some autographs and had his picture taken with the family. Hockey was Jarome's life, but friendliness was his passport to the world.

The next night it was all business for Jarome. If the Flames won, they would advance to the next round of the playoffs. If they lost, their season was over and the players would go home for the summer. Game 7 was the opposite of the previous game. This time, Jarome single-handedly took control of the outcome. He scored in the second and third periods to give Calgary a 2-0 lead. Jarome was winning every battle for the puck, creating one scoring chance after another, and doing everything possible to bring victory to the team. Still, the Canucks would not give up. They tied the game with two goals in the third to force the game into overtime. Jarome, though, was not going to lose.

In overtime, he came in over the blueline and fired a shot that goalie Alexander Auld saved. Jarome went to the net looking for the rebound, but Alex made that save as

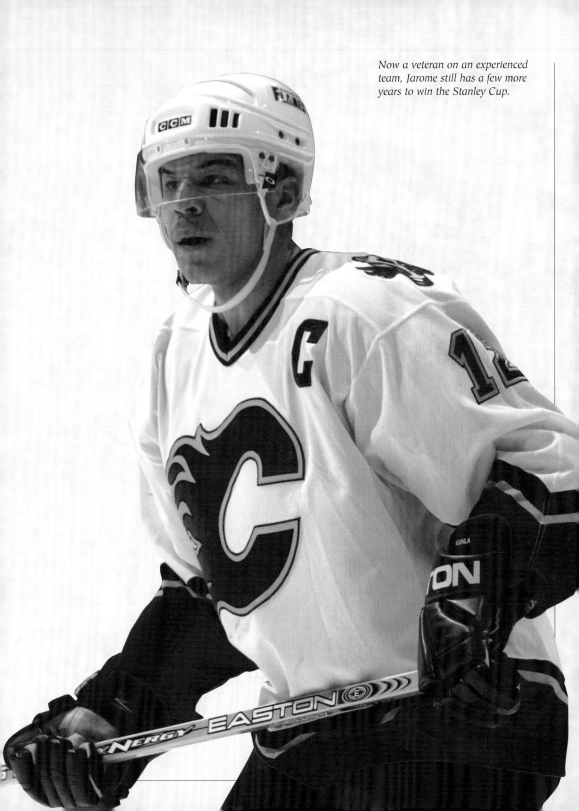

Now a veteran on an experienced team, Jarome still has a few more years to win the Stanley Cup.

During the pre-game warmup Jarome skates without a helmet, but once the game starts for real he wears both helmet and visor for safety.

well. Calgary teammate Martin Gelinas scooped the rebound into the net, though, and the Flames won the game and the series. "In my 25 years of hockey," coach Sutter said referring to Jarome's great game, "that was the single most dominant game I've ever seen a player play."

The series win was the first time Calgary had won a playoff round since 1989. That year, the team won the Stanley Cup. But their task was only going to be more difficult because their next opponent was the Detroit Red Wings, one of the absolute best teams in the league. And again, Calgary would not have home ice advantage, meaning that four of the seven possible games would be played in Detroit.

Still, Calgary came out and played another amazing game to begin the series. This time, they won 2-1 thanks to an overtime goal by Marcus Nilson. The win gave Calgary a 1-0 lead in the series and also gave the team extra confidence. The team lost the second game 5-2, though. Jarome was watched extra closely by the Red Wings and wasn't very effective that game. "He's one of the best players in the world," Detroit goalie Curtis Joseph noted, "so we have to be aware when he's on the ice."

Jarome got free in Game 3 long enough to score another crucial goal. With the game tied 1-1, he fought hard in the corner to maintain possession of the puck. He passed off to Martin Gelinas and then went hard to the net, and Martin passed right back to him. Jarome fired a great shot before Curtis Joseph could react, and the Flames had a 2-1 lead. They went on to win, 3-2.

Detroit tied the series two nights later, but Jarome and Craig Conroy connected again in Game 5 to give the Flames another critical 3-2 series lead. In that game, Jarome made a great pass to his linemate in the slot, and Craig fired home the goal late in the second period. It was the only goal of the tight 1-0 win for Calgary. As it turned out, the Flames lost game six but won game seven right in Detroit to advance to the Conference finals against the San Jose Sharks. The winner would go on to play for the Stanley Cup.

Again, the Flames opened the series on the road. Again, they started with a victory. And again, yes, it was Jarome at one end and Miikka Kiprusoff at the other who were the reasons for the win. The game was tied 3-3 after regulation, and late in the overtime "Kipper" made two great saves on Sharks players. The Flames then brought the puck into the San Jose end. Jarome held onto the puck in the slot until defenceman Steve Montador got into a good position. Jarome made the perfect pass, and Steve scored the winning goal with a great blast.

The Flames were on their way to another hard-fought series win, and Jarome scored a goal in all four of Calgary's wins. And, in the two games the team lost, he was held without a goal.

In the deciding game of the series, Jarome scored the first goal and teammate Martin Gelinas scored the second. San Jose made it close, 2-1, but the Sharks couldn't get the tying goal and the Flames scored into an empty net at the end to make it 3-1. Calgary won the series in six games, and the Flames were now headed to a best-of-seven showdown against Tampa Bay for the Stanley Cup! "You never know when this opportunity is going to come again in your life," an excited Jarome said during the dressing room celebrations after the big win.

He would enjoy this night, and in the morning he would work on his lifetime dream—winning the Stanley Cup.

"This is what sports is about," Jarome said with a big smile. "You get in big games, and you have a chance to win, a chance to win a series. A chance to win the final prize."

Jarome skates into the opposition end to forecheck the puck carrier and pressure him to make an error.

STANLEY CUP
GAME SEVEN

CHAPTER SIX

Jarome is stopped by Detroit goalie Curtis Joseph on a breakaway.

"We all know this is going to be
our last game of the season."

*Jarome, prior to Game Seven of
the 2004 Stanley Cup finals*

It's every boy's dream to play in the Stanley Cup finals, and now Jarome's dream was coming true. Of course, he never would have guessed at the beginning of the year that the team could go so far, but now that it was here, he didn't want to settle for second best—he wanted the Cup now!

In Game 1, in Tampa Bay, Jarome again powered the team to victory, this time a convincing 4-1 win. He scored the second Calgary goal to give his team a 2-0 lead on a great breakaway, but the whole game he led by example. He made several great hits, drove hard to the net, and seemed to be a man on a mission. The Flames lost the second game by the same 4-1 score, but they had the advantage heading home to Calgary for Games 3 and 4.

Jarome had a Gordie Howe hat trick in the third game to lead his team to victory and into a 2-1 series lead. He set up Chris Simon for the opening goal of the game, scored late in the third period to make the score 3-0, and he got into a fight with Tampa Bay forward Vincent Lecavalier early in the game to prove his team's toughness. Fighting isn't usually a part of Jarome's game, but on this night he helped bring his teammates to life by taking on the Lightning's best player. The rest of the night Jarome had fire in his eyes while Vincent was never a factor for his team.

The rest of the night Jarome had fire in his eyes while Vincent was never a factor for his team.

Tampa Bay bounced right back and won Game 4 by the slimmest of margins, 1-0. Game 5 was tense from start to finish because the winning team would take a 3-2 lead in the series and have a chance to win the Cup the very next game. Yet again, it was captain Jarome who made the difference in the game. With the score tied 1-1 early in the second period, Jarome blew down the right wing and hammered a hard slapshot that off the far post and past Nikolai Khabibulin to give the Flames a 2-1 lead.

Tampa Bay tied the game in the third to send the game into overtime, but Jarome was not going to lose. Midway through the first extra period he had perhaps the best shift of the entire playoffs. He was fighting for puck control behind the Tampa net, losing his helmet in the process. He got the puck, skated out in front with his back to the goal and then spun around quickly and took a shot. The puck hit the goalie in the chest, but Jarome's teammate Oleg Saprykin scooped the loose puck into the goal to give the Flames an amazing 3-2 win! Calgary was going home for Game 6 —and the Stanley Cup would be in the building, waiting for the Flames to claim if they could win one more game.

Tampa scored first in Game 6 but the Flames tied the score later in the first period. The same thing happened in the second, and the third period was dominated by the Flames as they could feel victory. In a tie game, just one goal would give them the Cup. But Tampa Bay goalie Nikolai Khabibulin stopped Jarome and his teammates time and again, and the game went into overtime again. The first extra period saw lots of scoring chances but no goals, but early in the fifth period of hockey it was Martin St. Louis who scored the winning goal for Tampa Bay to force a seventh and final game.

"I wasn't very good," Jarome said of his Game 6 performance. "But I'm excited now…We all know this is going to be our last game of the season. There's going to be nothing left on the table. This is what we've dreamed of."

Game 7. Stanley Cup finals. No dream gets better than this. The Cup was in the building, and it would be presented after the game. Everyone knew that. What no one knew was whether it would be presented to Jarome, as captain of Calgary, or Dave Andreychuk, as captain of Tampa.

Unfortunately, Calgary did not start the game as it would have liked. Tampa Bay skated and hit hard to establish a fast

Jarome gets around Vancouver defenceman Mattias Ohlund who tries to slow him down without incurring a penalty.

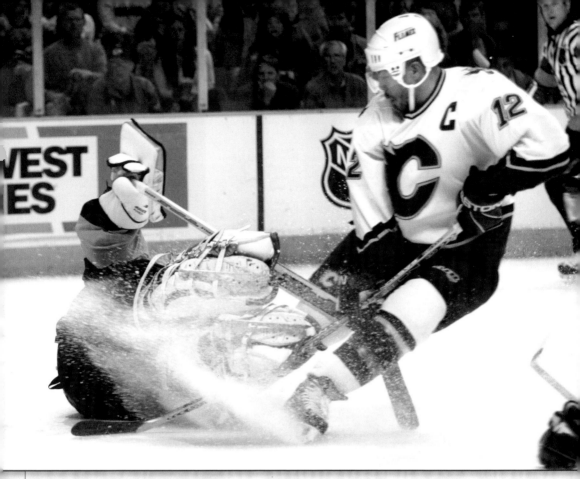

Jarome goes hard to the net with the puck, trying to force it in the goal through sheer will and strength.

tempo to the game, and the Lightning scored in the first and second to take a 2-1 lead. Craig Conroy scored for the Flames midway through the third to make it 2-1, but the Flames could not get the tying goal. It wasn't meant to be this year for Jarome. He started the year as captain, hoping to take the team to the playoffs, and he ended the year in tears in the dressing

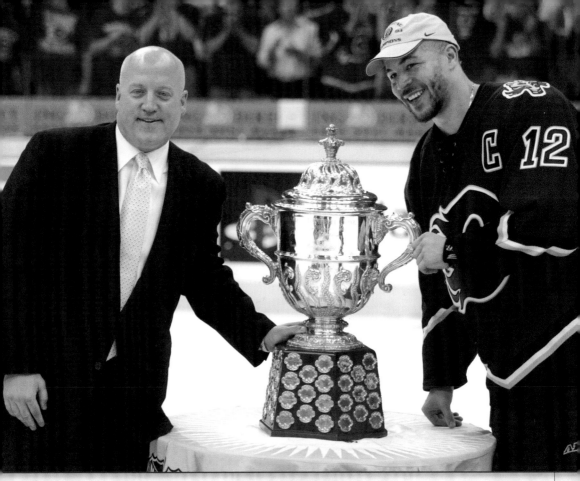

*Jarome receives the Clarence Campbell bowl from Bill Daly
of the NHL during Calgary's amazing Cup run in 2004.*

room after game seven of the Stanley Cup finals. It had been a great year, but when you get so close and lose, it can be heartbreaking. It was clear, though, that the decision to make him captain was the right one, and at 26 years of age Jarome would hopefully have plenty of time to take his team to Cup victory before he retired.

A SECOND OLYMPICS

Toronto defenceman Bryan McCabe tries to slow Jarome up at the blueline, but the Flames captain waits patiently to make a play.

"What really defines Jarome is his sense of right and wrong."

Jarome's grandfather, Elvis

That Game 7 moment was great for Jarome, but it wasn't easy to remember the good and forget the bad. "I would say it took a couple of months before it didn't hurt to think about it," he said many months later. "But at the same time, you have to look at what a great time it was and how fortunate you were to get to experience such an amazing playoff run. It was a great time for the city of Calgary. The end result wasn't there, but the dream run was unbelievable."

After that summer, Jarome attended training camp for a reunion of Team Canada's best players, this time for the 2004 World Cup of Hockey. It was a strange time in the game's history, though, because the day after that tournament was scheduled to end the contract between the NHL and the players expired. That meant that a great tournament was sure to be followed by a loss of hockey altogether because the two groups could not agree on so many business issues needed before the NHL could play games.

Still, Jarome came to Toronto for the World Cup and had the time of his life. Coach Pat Quinn played him on a line with Mario Lemieux and Joe Sakic, the best of the best, and Jarome looked just as good as his world-class linemates.

> "It was a great time for the city of Calgary. The end result wasn't there, but the dream run was unbelievable."

At the same time, Jarome was hired by the Canadian Imperial Bank of Commerce (CIBC) to do an important TV commercial for the company, a big step in making him more familiar to people right across the country. "It's my first national commercial," Jarome said with pride. "I'd love to see the game of hockey grow, and if there's anything I can do, it'd be fun."

Canada won the tournament with a close win over Finland in the finals, but after that there was no hockey for a full year

Soon enough, though, Jarome had the team on the winning track, and by the end of the calendar year the team was in first place.

and more. Still, Jarome was very busy. He and his wife had their first child in November 2004, and Jarome spent the rest of the year in Calgary training and working out, just not playing. The result was, "I was in great aerobic shape, but (lacked) a lot of explosion," Jarome explained.

Eventually the league and players agreed to a new contract and the NHL started up again for the 2005-06 season. Jarome picked up where he left off, as team captain, but after not playing for a full year it took him a while to get his legs, find his scoring touch, and lead the team. Still, all the elements of his leadership fell into place soon enough, and Calgary established itself as a playoff team once again.

The Flames won just three of their first nine games, and as usual Jarome started slowly. Soon enough, though, Jarome had the team on the winning track, and by the end of the calendar year the team was in first place in the Northwest Division. This was also an Olympic year, and just as in 1998 and 2002, the NHL was ready to take a break in February 2006 to allow the world's best players to participate for their countries at the Olympics. This year there was no doubt Jarome would be on the team, and just as the break was nearing Jarome started to pick up his scoring with the Flames.

Unfortunately, this year's edition of Team Canada didn't fare so well in Turin, Italy, where the Olympics were played. Canada got off to a slow start and never gained confidence, and as a result the team was eliminated in the quarter-finals. Jarome scored just twice, but he came home focused on helping the Flames improve as they moved toward the playoffs.

By the end of the regular season, the team was still on top of its division, finishing with 103 points. Jarome finished the year

Jarome played for Canada at the 2004 World Cup of Hockey.

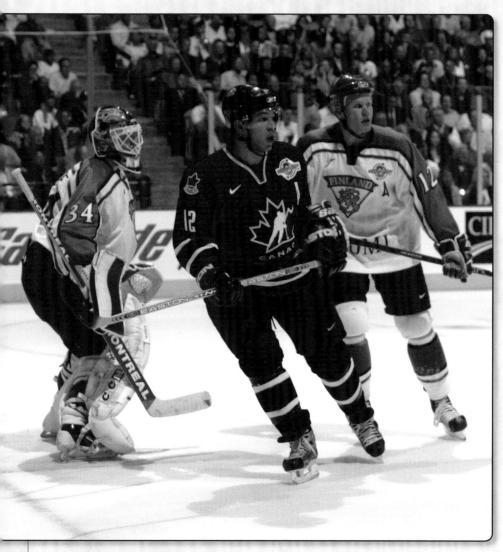

Jarome goes to the front of the Finnish goal during the World Cup finals won by Canada.

The Sensational Jarome Iginla

Jarome handles the puck against Finland in the championship game of the World Cup at Air Canada Centre, Toronto.

Jarome holds high the unique trophy, designed by world-famous architect Frank Gehry.

with 35 goals, and the Flames were set to face the Mighty Ducks of Anaheim in a first-round playoff matchup. This was not an easy series. Calgary won the first game, then the Ducks won game two. The Flames won game three, and in the next game it was Anaheim again by a 3-2 score. Jarome scored both Calgary goals in the third period to try to ignite a rally, but the team fell just short.

In game five, Jarome was the hero. He scored the team's second and third goals, and this time it was the Flames that won 3-2 to take a big 3-2 lead in the series. That was the last of Jarome and the team this season. Anaheim came back to win the final two games and eliminate the Flames, and Jarome went home to get ready for another year.

The 2005-06 season was a long one for him, frustrating because the team didn't go as far in the playoffs and he wasn't able to help Canada win at the Olympics. Of course, you can't win them all, but if anyone ever tried to win them all, it was Jarome. A superstar player on ice and a superstar person off it, the Flames and his fans knew he'd be back with even more desire to win the next season.

> *Of course, you can't win them all, but if anyone ever tried to win them all, it was Jarome.*

Jarome Iginla by the Numbers

Jarome Iginla
b. Edmonton, Alberta, July 1, 1977
6'1", 208 lbs., shoots right

Drafted 11th overall by Dallas at 1995 Entry Draft
Traded to Calgary with Corey Millen for Joe
Nieuwendyk on December 19, 1995

Provincial Junior

Year	Team	GP	G	A	P	Pim
1991-92	St. Albert	36	26	30	56	22
1992-93	St. Albert	36	34	53	87	20

Western Hockey League

Year	Team	GP	G	A	P	Pim
1993-94	Kamloops	48	6	23	29	33
1994-95	Kamloops	72	33	38	71	111
1995-96	Kamloops	63	63	73	136	120

NHL, Regular Season

Year	Team	GP	G	A	P	Pim
1995-96	Calgary	DNP				
1996-97	Calgary	82	21	29	50	37
1997-98	Calgary	70	13	19	32	29
1998-99	Calgary	82	28	32	51	58
1999-00	Calgary	77	29	34	63	26
2000-01	Calgary	77	31	40	71	62
2001-02	Calgary	82	52	44	96	77
2002-03	Calgary	75	35	32	67	49
2003-04	Calgary	81	41	32	73	84
2004-05		NO SEASON				
2005-06	Calgary	82	35	32	67	86
Totals	9 years	708	285	285	570	508

Jarome poses with Canada's prime minister,
Paul Martin, in the Flames' dressing room.

The look of intensity and determination says it all—
Jarome plays to win every shift.

NHL, Playoffs

Year	Team	GP	G	A	P	Pim
1995-96	Calgary	2	1	1	2	0
1996-97	Calgary	DNQ				
1997-98	Calgary	DNQ				
1999-00	Calgary	DNQ				
2000-01	Calgary	DNQ				
2001-02	Calgary	DNQ				
2002-03	Calgary	DNQ				
2003-04	Calgary	26	13	9	22	45
2004-05	NO SEASON					
2005-06	Calgary	7	5	3	8	11
Totals	3 years	35	19	13	32	56

International

Year	Team	GP	G	A	P	Pim	Finish
1996	WJC	6	5	7	12	4	Gold
1997	WC	11	2	3	5	2	Gold
2002	OLY	6	3	1	4	0	Gold
2004	WCH	6	2	1	3	2	First
2006	OLY	6	2	1	3	4	7th

WJC–World Junior Championship
WC–World Championship
OLY–Olympics
WCH–World Cup of Hockey

ACKNOWLEDGEMENTS

This book couldn't have happened without publisher Jordan Fenn, who has embraced my work since day one. Thanks are also due to the superb design team of Michael Gray and Rob Scanlan at First Image. Also to Craig Campbell, Phil Pritchard, Danielle Siciliano, and Miragh Addis at the Hockey Hall of Fame, and to David Pillinger and Nancy Glowinski at Reuters.

PHOTO CREDITS

Dave Sandford/Hockey Hall of Fame—p. 25 (bottom), 27 (top), 34-35, 36, 42, 45, 55, 57, 68, 71, 72, 74, 78

Dave Sandford/Hockey Canada—p. 32, 41

Dave Sandford/IIHF—p. 39, 40

Reuters—p. 62, 65, 66, 67, 76

Andy Devlin/Hockey Hall of Fame—p. 46, 48, 51, 52, 58, 61

Matthew Manor/Hockey Hall of Fame—p. 4, 6, 73

Doug MacLellan/Hockey Hall of Fame—p. 17, 19, 24

Ottawa Senators/Hockey Hall of Fame—p. 20, 25 (top)

David Klutho/Hockey Hall of Fame—p. 23, 28-29, 30

Chris Relke/Hockey Hall of Fame—p. 12, 15, 16

Steve Babineau/Hockey Hall of Fame—p. 27 (bottom)

Paul Bereswill/Hockey Hall of Fame—p. 9, 10